December Holidays

Preschool/Kindergarten

Save time and energy planning thematic units with this comprehensive resource. We've searched through the 1990–1997 issues of **The MAILBOX®** and **Teacher's Helper®** magazines to find the best ideas for you to use when teaching during December holidays. Included in this book are favorite units from the magazines, single ideas to extend a unit, and a variety of reproducible activities. Use these season pleasin' activities to develop your own complete unit or simply to enhance your current lesson plans. You're sure to find everything you need for festive holiday learning.

Editors:
Angie Kutzer
Thad H. McLaurin
Michele M. Stoffel Menzel

Artists:
Pam Crane
Kimberly Richard

Cover Artist:
Kimberly Richard

www.themailbox.com

©2000 by THE EDUCATION CENTER, INC.
All rights reserved.
ISBN# 1-56234-358-0

Manufactured in the United States
10 9 8 7 6 5 4 3

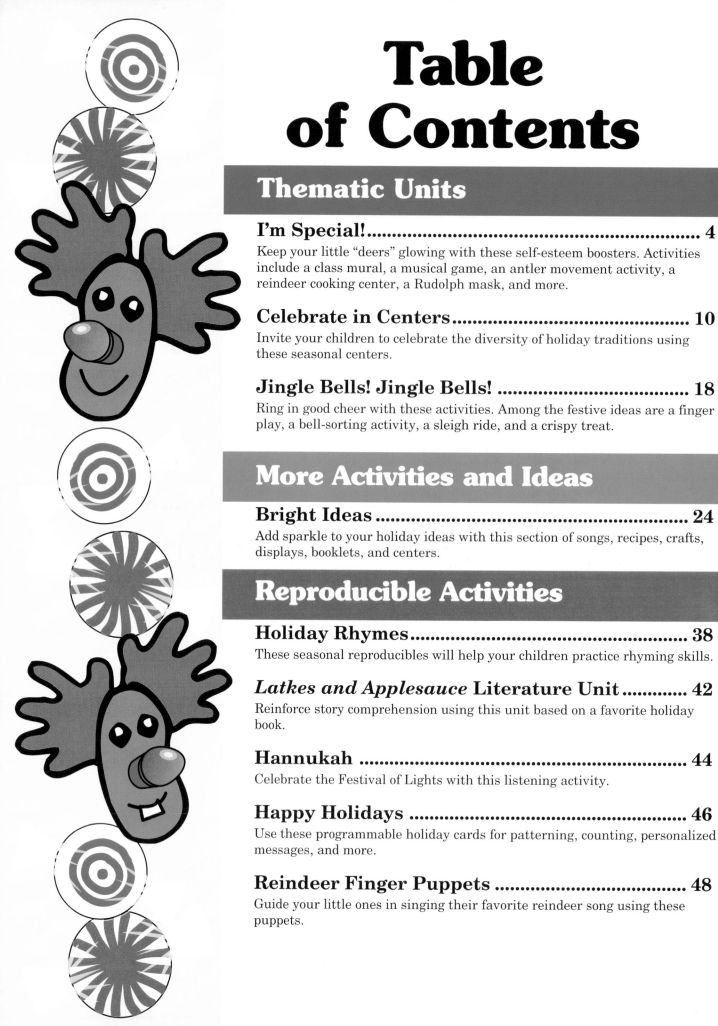

Table of Contents

Thematic Units

More Activities and Ideas

Reproducible Activities

Thematic Units...

from The MAILBOX® magazine

I'm Special!

Like Rudolph, children who believe in themselves can rise to any occasion. Sometimes it just takes a Santa Claus to point out a child's potential and lead her in the right direction. Use these self-esteem boosters to keep your little "deers" glowing!

ideas contributed by Kerry Rogers

The Most Famous Reindeer Of All

You'll go down in history when you don a pair of paper antlers (see the directions on page 6), tape a red circle on your nose, and read aloud a version of Rudolph's well-loved story. If possible, share the original story by Robert L. May. Then lead your group in singing "Rudolph The Red-Nosed Reindeer" as made famous by Gene Autry. Help your little ones understand that even though we're different on the outside, it's what's inside—the attitudes we have about ourselves—that makes us really special!

We all are special as can be;
You are you, and I am me.
Looking different matters not;
It's what's inside that counts a lot!

susan hodnett

Everyone Is Special

Use this song to make each and every child feel special. Seat youngsters in a group circle. In turn, place the previously used antler headband and nose on a child in the group. Then sing the first verse of the following song to point out one of that child's special characteristics. For example, you could sing, "…who has curly hair," "…with a dimple in her chin," or "…who likes to use paint." Then ask the group to join you in singing the second verse. Be careful not to compare children's abilities, but to bring out each child's unique traits. Yes, we know somebody special!

Somebody Special
(sung to the tune of "Have You Ever Seen A Lassie?")

Do you know somebody special, so special, so special?
Do you know somebody special [child's unique trait]?

Yes, we know somebody special, so special, so special.
Yes, we know somebody special, (and) his/her name is [child's name].

Unique Reflections

One sure way to make a child feel special is to ask her to spend some time with you! In turn, invite each child to stand with you near a full-length mirror. Ask her to name an aspect of her appearance that makes her special. Write "I'm Special!" and her response on a sheet of construction paper. Next help her identify some aspect of her personality or an ability that makes her special. Record this thought on the paper also. To complete the page, ask the child to sit near the mirror as she draws her self-portrait.

Darling Deer

Your little dears' portraits will look darling when posted with these reindeer projects. Ask each child to cut a heart shape out of tan construction paper. Next trace the child's hands onto a sheet of brown paper; then cut them out. Direct the child to glue the hand shapes to the heart as shown to resemble antlers, draw a smile, and add wiggle eyes and a pom-pom nose. Invite each child to personalize her deer by decorating it with her choice of materials, such as ribbons, wrapping paper, or holiday decorations. Finally, glue a spring-type clothespin to the back of the deer. Secure the child's portrait in the clip before displaying both projects.

I'm special!

I have dimples!

Charles

I know just when you need a hug!

Rudolph and I are both special, you see;
My hands and feet only match me!

Lizzy

Reindeer Roundup

When Rudolph got a chance to guide Santa's sleigh, he put his best foot forward. Give your little ones a chance to put their best *feet* and *hands* forward with this class mural. To make a Rudolph print, a child dips his foot in a shallow pan of brown paint, then presses it onto a length of bulletin-board paper. After washing his foot clean, he then dips the palm sides of both hands into the paint, then presses them above the footprint as shown to resemble antlers. When his hands are clean, he dips a thumb in red paint, then presses it onto the footprint to resemble a nose. After washing his hand once again, he glues paper or wiggle eyes to the reindeer. Write his name or attach his picture near his print. When the mural is complete, display it within children's reach along with the rhyme shown. Encourage youngsters to find their classmates' handprints on the mural.

Won't You Guide My Sleigh Tonight?

It's time to follow the leader—reindeer style! In advance of this movement activity, locate a recorded version of "Rudolph The Red-Nosed Reindeer." Then prepare an antler headband for each child. To make one, trace both of a child's hands side by side near the top of a large piece of brown paper. Cut on the resulting outlines, leaving a strip of paper below the hand shapes as shown. Fit each child's antler headband on his head; then staple the ends of the band together.

During a group time, ask each child to don his headband; then line up the reindeer in an obstacle-free space. Together try various types of reindeer movements such as walking, running, leaping, jumping, galloping, and prancing. Invite a child to lead the group in any movement of his choice as you play the song. After an appropriate time, stop the song, and invite a different child to be the leader. Repeat until each child has an opportunity to lead the herd. Hey, Santa! Can I guide your sleigh in my own special way?

Pockets Of Praise

Help each child make one of these dashing reindeer pockets; then use your sharing times to fill each child's pocket with praise for all his special traits. Have each child paint the front of one paper plate and the back of half a plate brown. When the paint is dry, staple the plates together to create a pocket. Trace the child's hands onto construction paper; then cut out the resulting outlines. Have him glue the hands onto the back of the pocket to resemble antlers. Glue large paper or wiggle eyes to the plate, along with a paper nose. Add a smile; then personalize each child's reindeer's nose. Display the pockets near your group area. Further prepare by duplicating a quantity of the "I'm Special!" note on page 9.

During a group time, select a child to be the focus of attention. Begin by suggesting several ways in which that child is special. Then request that several classmates add to the list. Write each characteristic on a separate "I'm Special!" note. Then drop the notes in the child's pocket. Continue for several group times, until you have filled each child's pocket with notes. If desired, add additional notes to the pockets as you and the class continue to observe each other's uniqueness. Finally, send each child's pocket home along with the parent note (page 9) and a supply of blank "I'm Special!" notes.

Hidden Talent

This circle-time activity is so much fun, your reindeer will shout with glee! In advance, prepare a Rudolph mask by painting a large paper bag as shown. Cut two antlers from tagboard; then attach them to the back of the bag. During a group time, ask youngsters to close their eyes. Then place the paper-bag reindeer over a child's head and shoulders. Ask the group to open their eyes; then give clues about the mystery student by describing ways that he is special. Play until each child's hidden talent is discovered!

A "Pear" Of Reindeer

Invite a pair of children to visit a cooking center to prepare a pair of reindeer. In the center, place pretzels and a variety of small items, such as colorful candy pieces, raisins, gumdrops, grape halves, cherries, and miniature marshmallows. Provide each child with a pear half on a plate. Direct each child to put two pretzel pieces into his pear. Then invite him to put his choice of the items on the pear to resemble eyes and a nose. Before the partners eat, compare the treats. They might look different, but they're both delicious!

Success Stories

Fly away with these additional stories about characters with star appeal.

Tacky The Penguin
Written by Helen Lester
Illustrated by Lynn Munsinger
Published by Houghton Mifflin Company

Dumbo
(Share your favorite version.)

Otto Is Different
Written by Franz Brandenberg
Illustrated by James Stevenson
Published by Greenwillow Books
(Check your library.)

The following suggestions for making kids feel special have been teacher tested and Rudolph approved!

No Two Are Alike

This creative project is a reminder that no two snowflakes—or children—are alike. Prepare a shallow tray of white paint. Direct each child to dip a hand into the paint, then press his hand onto a sheet of blue construction paper so that his palm print is in the center of the page. Have him continue in this manner, printing his palm in the center each time, while moving the location of the fingerprints to create the six points of a snowflake. Have him sprinkle the flake with clear glitter. When the paint is dry, cut around the shape of the flake; then use white chalk to personalize the back of it. Punch a hole in each flake; then hang the flakes from the ceiling with clear fishing line.

Bonnie McKenzie—Pre-K And Gr. K
Cheshire Country Day School
Cheshire, CT

Royal Abilities

This musical game is sure to make every child feel like a king or queen. To prepare, make a crown and decorate a chair to resemble a throne. Arrange the same number of chairs (including the throne) as there are children playing the game in a large circle. Begin play by directing the students to walk in a line inside the circle in a manner similar to Musical Chairs. Stop the music and direct the children to be seated. Place the crown on the child seated on the throne. Then request that several children in the group say a positive thought about that child. For example, a child might say, "You're a king at painting pictures," or "You're a queen at building with blocks." Continue play until each child has had an opportunity to sit on the throne. Now that's the royal treatment!

Sharon Wicklein
Belleville, IL

I Can!

You can really boost a child's self-esteem with this idea! Cut a supply of construction-paper strips that measure 1½" x 7". Keep the strips and some small stickers handy. Then, when you observe a child doing something special, label a strip "I can!" and describe the achievement. Suggest that the child choose a sticker to decorate the strip. Wrap the strip around his wrist to resemble a bracelet; then tape the ends together.

Jennifer Casstevens—Preschool
West Yadkin Headstart
Hamptonville, NC

:) "I can!"
Miriam can help clean up!

:) "I can!"
Miriam can help clean up!

I'm Special!

Dear Parent,

Like Rudolph, children who believe in themselves can rise to any occasion. Inside this pocket you'll find notes describing ways that your child's classmates and I believe she/he is special. Please write more special characteristics on the blank notes. Then watch your child GLOW!

Up, up, and away,
I can fly so high!
Just believe in me,
And I'll reach for the sky!

9

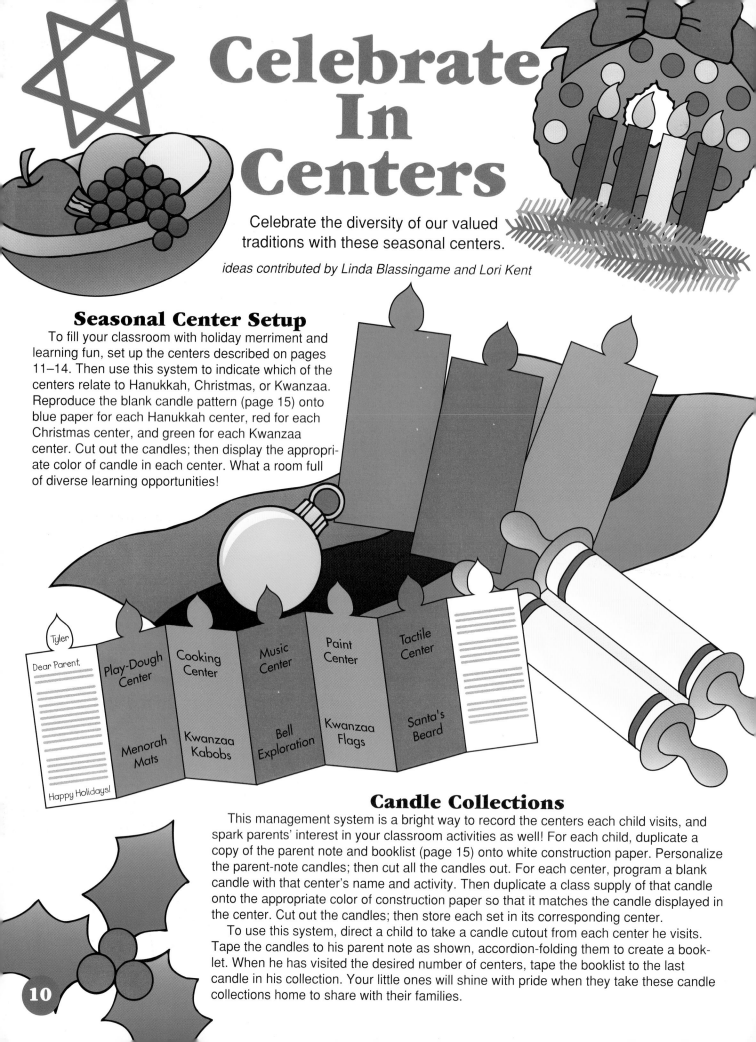

Celebrate In Centers

Celebrate the diversity of our valued traditions with these seasonal centers.

ideas contributed by Linda Blassingame and Lori Kent

Seasonal Center Setup

To fill your classroom with holiday merriment and learning fun, set up the centers described on pages 11–14. Then use this system to indicate which of the centers relate to Hanukkah, Christmas, or Kwanzaa. Reproduce the blank candle pattern (page 15) onto blue paper for each Hanukkah center, red for each Christmas center, and green for each Kwanzaa center. Cut out the candles; then display the appropriate color of candle in each center. What a room full of diverse learning opportunities!

Candle Collections

This management system is a bright way to record the centers each child visits, and spark parents' interest in your classroom activities as well! For each child, duplicate a copy of the parent note and booklist (page 15) onto white construction paper. Personalize the parent-note candles; then cut all the candles out. For each center, program a blank candle with that center's name and activity. Then duplicate a class supply of that candle onto the appropriate color of construction paper so that it matches the candle displayed in the center. Cut out the candles; then store each set in its corresponding center.

To use this system, direct a child to take a candle cutout from each center he visits. Tape the candles to his parent note as shown, accordion-folding them to create a booklet. When he has visited the desired number of centers, tape the booklist to the last candle in his collection. Your little ones will shine with pride when they take these candle collections home to share with their families.

Hanukkah

These centers focus on the Jewish holiday Hanukkah—the Festival of Lights.

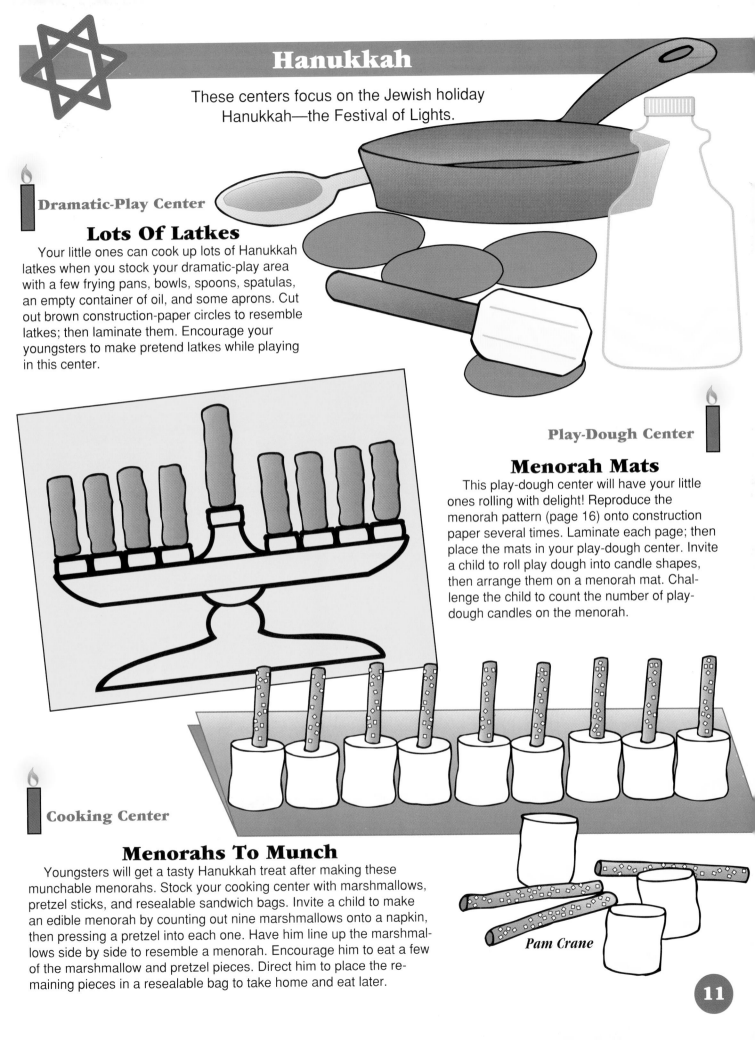

Dramatic-Play Center

Lots Of Latkes

Your little ones can cook up lots of Hanukkah latkes when you stock your dramatic-play area with a few frying pans, bowls, spoons, spatulas, an empty container of oil, and some aprons. Cut out brown construction-paper circles to resemble latkes; then laminate them. Encourage your youngsters to make pretend latkes while playing in this center.

Play-Dough Center

Menorah Mats

This play-dough center will have your little ones rolling with delight! Reproduce the menorah pattern (page 16) onto construction paper several times. Laminate each page; then place the mats in your play-dough center. Invite a child to roll play dough into candle shapes, then arrange them on a menorah mat. Challenge the child to count the number of play-dough candles on the menorah.

Cooking Center

Menorahs To Munch

Youngsters will get a tasty Hanukkah treat after making these munchable menorahs. Stock your cooking center with marshmallows, pretzel sticks, and resealable sandwich bags. Invite a child to make an edible menorah by counting out nine marshmallows onto a napkin, then pressing a pretzel into each one. Have him line up the marshmallows side by side to resemble a menorah. Encourage him to eat a few of the marshmallow and pretzel pieces. Direct him to place the remaining pieces in a resealable bag to take home and eat later.

Pam Crane

11

Your little elves will have a "ho, ho, ho" lot of fun celebrating Christmas in these jolly centers!

Woodworking Center

Santa's Workshop

Turn your woodworking center into Santa's workshop with the addition of Styrofoam® pieces, empty spools, craft sticks, glue, and markers. Provide toy catalogs to help your busy workers gather ideas. Encourage a child visiting this center to make a toy for Santa's sleigh using the materials provided. To add a little touch of elfin delight, provide students with felt Santa hats to wear while they are hard at work.

Tactile Center

Santa's Beard Is Soft And White

Your little merrymakers will get a real feel for Santa's beard when visiting this tactile center. Enlarge the Santa pattern (page 17) onto a large sheet of white paper. Color the pattern. Tape it onto a tabletop; then cover it with clear Con-Tact® covering. Squirt a dollop of nonmenthol-scented shaving cream onto Santa's beard. Invite a child to use her fingers to give Santa a beard that is fluffy and white.

Gross-Motor Center

Holiday Beanbag Toss

Use this idea to toss some gross-motor fun into your holiday centers. Use an X-acto® knife to cut a Christmas-tree shape out of a piece of green foam board. Cut circles from the tree to resemble ornaments. Hot-glue the tree shape to a cylindrical container filled with sand. Place the tree on the floor in an open area. Place several beanbags in a gift-wrapped box near the tree. Invite one child in a pair to toss a beanbag through a hole in the tree. Have his partner stand near the tree, righting it if it falls. When all the beanbags have been tossed, have the pair return them to the box. Then direct the pair to change roles.

Shelly Dohogne—Early Childhood Special Education
Scott County Central, Sikeston, MO

Invite your little angels to celebrate the Advent season in these centers.

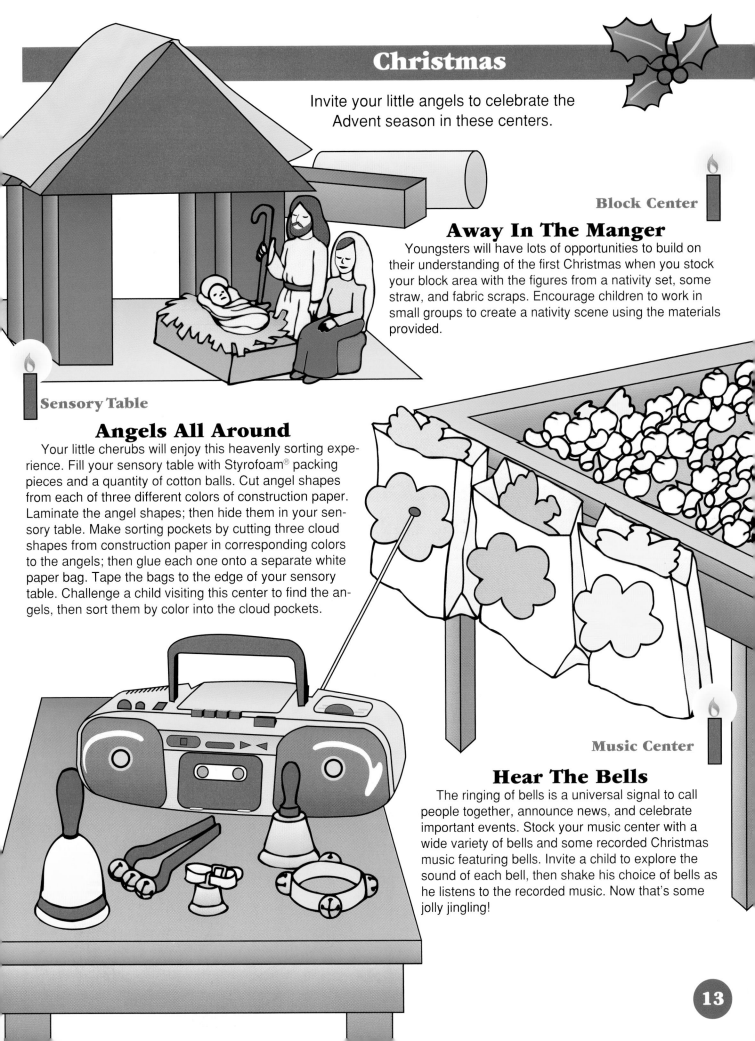

Block Center

Away In The Manger

Youngsters will have lots of opportunities to build on their understanding of the first Christmas when you stock your block area with the figures from a nativity set, some straw, and fabric scraps. Encourage children to work in small groups to create a nativity scene using the materials provided.

Sensory Table

Angels All Around

Your little cherubs will enjoy this heavenly sorting experience. Fill your sensory table with Styrofoam® packing pieces and a quantity of cotton balls. Cut angel shapes from each of three different colors of construction paper. Laminate the angel shapes; then hide them in your sensory table. Make sorting pockets by cutting three cloud shapes from construction paper in corresponding colors to the angels; then glue each one onto a separate white paper bag. Tape the bags to the edge of your sensory table. Challenge a child visiting this center to find the angels, then sort them by color into the cloud pockets.

Music Center

Hear The Bells

The ringing of bells is a universal signal to call people together, announce news, and celebrate important events. Stock your music center with a wide variety of bells and some recorded Christmas music featuring bells. Invite a child to explore the sound of each bell, then shake his choice of bells as he listens to the recorded music. Now that's some jolly jingling!

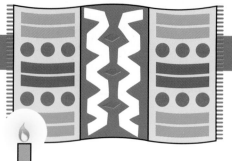

Kwanzaa

At these centers students can celebrate the values and traditions of African-Americans.

Paint Center

Kwanzaa Flags

Your little ones will learn the colors of Kwanzaa when making *benderas,* or flags. Stock your easel with large sheets of white construction paper and red, green, and black paint. Encourage a child to paint a flag as shown. When the paint is dry, tape his flag to a paint-stirring stick for a handle. When each child's flag is complete, lead students in a parade around the classroom as you play some traditional African music. Happy Kwanzaa!

Cooking Center

Kwanzaa Kabobs

Students will love preparing these delicious fruit kabobs to remind them of the bountiful harvest celebrated during Kwanzaa. In your cooking center, place a variety of fruit pieces such as pineapple, apples, bananas, oranges, and maraschino cherries. Add black paper plates and a supply of red and green toothpicks. Invite a small group of children to visit the center. Direct each child to skewer her choice of fruits onto red and green toothpicks to make kabobs. Then have her place her kabobs on a plate. When each child has prepared her kabobs, invite the group to sit together to celebrate the harvest.

Manipulative Center

African Trading Beads

To prepare this center, dye quantities of penne pasta red and green. Mix several drops of red or green food coloring with enough rubbing alcohol to soak the amount of pasta you would like to dye that color. Soak the pasta; then drain it before spreading it out to dry. Place the dry pasta and lengths of black yarn in a center. Encourage a child to string the pasta onto the yarn; then knot the ends together to form a necklace.

Hanukkah!
Written by Roni Schotter
Published by Little, Brown And Company; 1993

The Christmas Alphabet
Written by Robert Sabuda
Published by Orchard Books, 1994

Santa's Favorite Story
Written by Hisako Aoki
Published by Simon & Schuster Children's Books, 1991

A Kwanzaa Celebration—A Pop-Up Book
Written by Nancy Williams
Published by Simon & Schuster Children's Books, 1995

©The Education Center, Inc.

Dear Parent,

We've been celebrating holiday traditions in our learning centers.

Unfold this booklet to see color-coded candles that name the centers your child participated in. Blue candles represent activities related to Hanukkah, red candles represent Christmas, and green candles represent Kwanzaa.

Ask your child to share some of his/her favorite activities. Then start a tradition of your own by visiting a library or bookstore to find the books listed on the last candle.

Happy Holidays!

©The Education Center, Inc.

Menorah Pattern

Use with "Menorah Mats" on page 11.

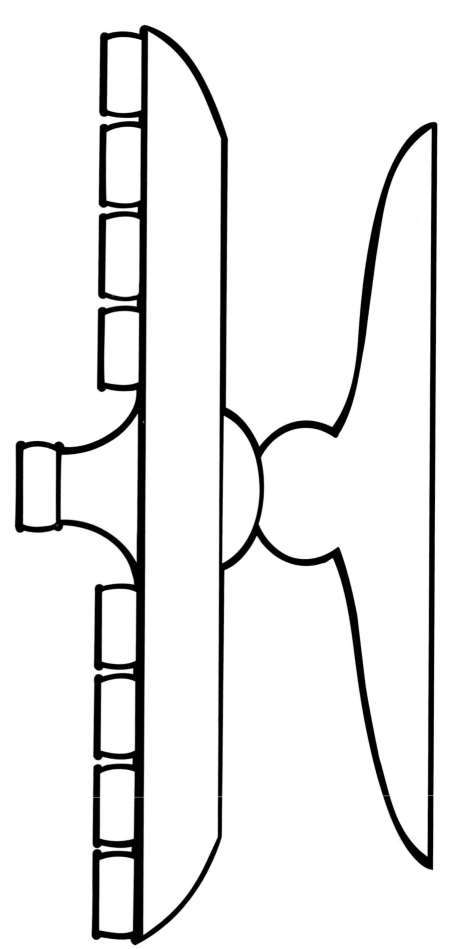

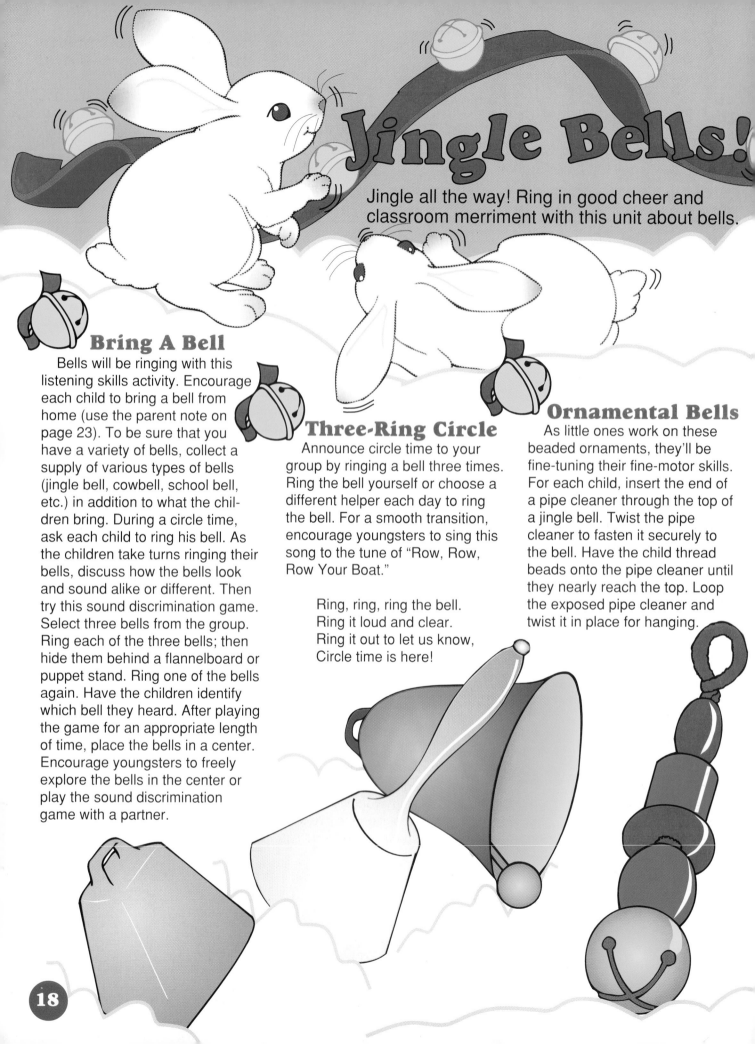

Jingle Bells!

Jingle all the way! Ring in good cheer and classroom merriment with this unit about bells.

Bring A Bell

Bells will be ringing with this listening skills activity. Encourage each child to bring a bell from home (use the parent note on page 23). To be sure that you have a variety of bells, collect a supply of various types of bells (jingle bell, cowbell, school bell, etc.) in addition to what the children bring. During a circle time, ask each child to ring his bell. As the children take turns ringing their bells, discuss how the bells look and sound alike or different. Then try this sound discrimination game. Select three bells from the group. Ring each of the three bells; then hide them behind a flannelboard or puppet stand. Ring one of the bells again. Have the children identify which bell they heard. After playing the game for an appropriate length of time, place the bells in a center. Encourage youngsters to freely explore the bells in the center or play the sound discrimination game with a partner.

Three-Ring Circle

Announce circle time to your group by ringing a bell three times. Ring the bell yourself or choose a different helper each day to ring the bell. For a smooth transition, encourage youngsters to sing this song to the tune of "Row, Row, Row Your Boat."

Ring, ring, ring the bell.
Ring it loud and clear.
Ring it out to let us know,
Circle time is here!

Ornamental Bells

As little ones work on these beaded ornaments, they'll be fine-tuning their fine-motor skills. For each child, insert the end of a pipe cleaner through the top of a jingle bell. Twist the pipe cleaner to fasten it securely to the bell. Have the child thread beads onto the pipe cleaner until they nearly reach the top. Loop the exposed pipe cleaner and twist it in place for hanging.

Jingle Bells!

Ideas contributed by Jean Huff—Four-Year-Olds, Bethel Presbyterian Weekday Program, Cornelius, NC, and Eva Murdock—Preschool, Children's Center, Shenandoah Baptist Church, Roanoke, VA

Jingle Bell Rock

Make these bells to ensure all of your little ones have their own bells to ring during group movement and music activities. Cut bell shapes from poster board. Have students decorate the bell shapes with markers; then laminate them, if desired. Hot glue a jingle bell to the bottom of each bell shape and a craft stick to the back of the bell shape. As you play a selection of lively holiday music, encourage youngsters to shake their bells. Get ready for jingle bell rock!

Jingle Bells Rhythm

Jiggle out the wiggles—and strengthen rhythm and listening skills—with this echo chant. Chant a line of the poem, ringing a jingle bell to keep a steady beat as indicated. Direct the children to copy your words and actions. After completing the poem once, ring your bell one to five times, counting aloud as you ring. Then have the children copy you by ringing and counting the same number of times.

▼   ▼   ▼   ▼
(Teacher:) Hear the mu-sic.

▼   ▼   ▼
Use your ears.

▼   ▼   ▼   ▼
Now re-peat just

▼   ▼   ▼
What you hear.

▼   ▼   ▼   ▼
(Children:) Hear the mu-sic.

▼   ▼   ▼
Use your ears.

▼   ▼   ▼   ▼
Now re-peat just

▼   ▼   ▼
What you hear.

Jingle, Jingle, Little Bells

Youngsters will enjoy singing and ringing to this jingle bell tune. Give each child a bell as described in "Jingle Bell Rock." As the class sings this song, encourage them to use the bells to accompany the suggested actions.

(sung to the tune of "Twinkle, Twinkle, Little Star")

Jingle, jingle, little bell.
I can ring my little bell.
Ring it high.
Ring it low.
Ring it fast.
Ring it slow.
Jingle, jingle, little bell.
I can ring my little bell.

Jingle, jingle, little bell.
I can ring my little bell.
Ring it left.
Ring it right.
Even ring it
Out of sight.
Jingle, jingle, little bell.
I can ring my little bell.

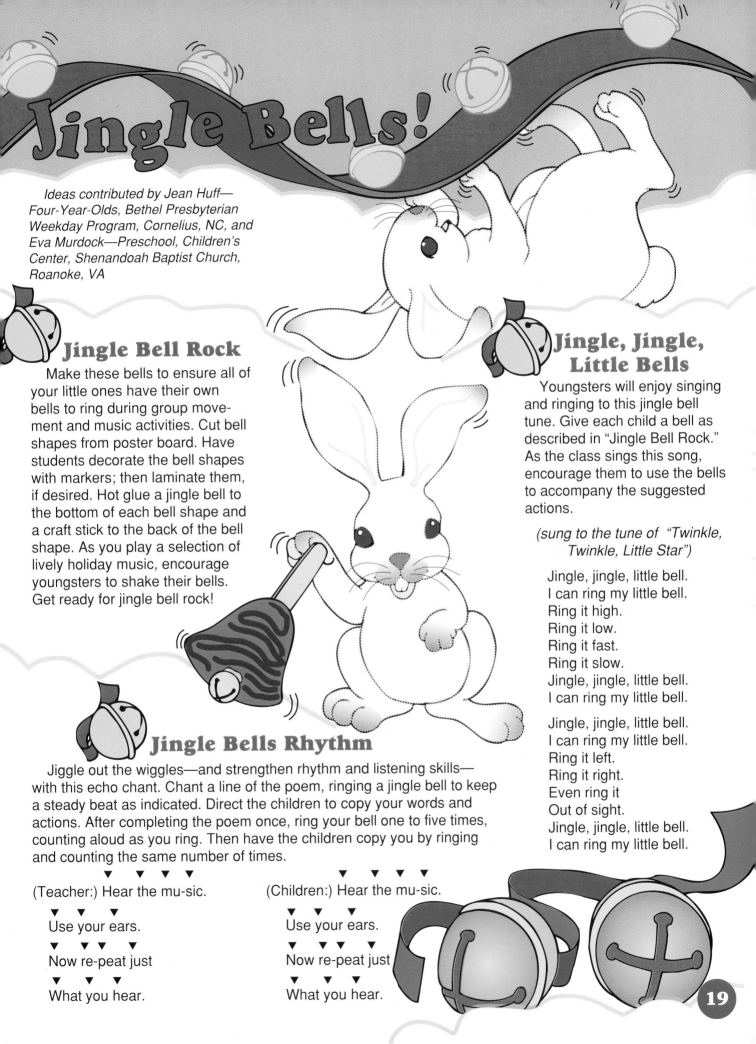

Bells In Baskets

Visit a craft store during the holiday season and you are sure to find a variety of bells. Purchase several colors and sizes of bells and store them in baskets. Encourage children to sort the bells by color, size, and loudness. Also assist children in counting sets of bells.

Cinnamon-Bread Bells

Ingredients:
1 slice of bread per child
a tub of margarine
cinnamon-sugar mixture in a shaker

For a tasty treat, have your little ones make cinnamon-bread bells. In advance place a toaster oven in your classroom housekeeping area. For each child, cut and personalize a square of aluminum foil that is slightly larger than a bell-shaped cookie cutter. Invite a small group of children to the center. Using the cookie cutter, have each child cut a bell shape from a piece of bread. Have him place his shape on his foil square. Next have him spread margarine over the shape and sprinkle it with the cinnamon-sugar mixture. Place the shapes in the oven and bake. Once the bread has cooled, invite youngsters to sit down at your housekeeping center table and enjoy!

Silver Bells

Use pears, paint, paper, and glitter to create these beautiful silver bells. Place several damp paper towels in a tray or pan. Spread white tempera paint over the paper towels. Slice a pear lengthwise, almost to the center. Slice the rounded bottom off the pear, leaving a piece in the center to resemble the bell clapper. Invite each child to press the pear into the paint and then onto construction paper. Have her continue in this manner until she has the desired number of prints on her paper. While the paint is wet, have her sprinkle glitter over the prints. Allow the prints to dry; then shake off the excess glitter.

Mopsy

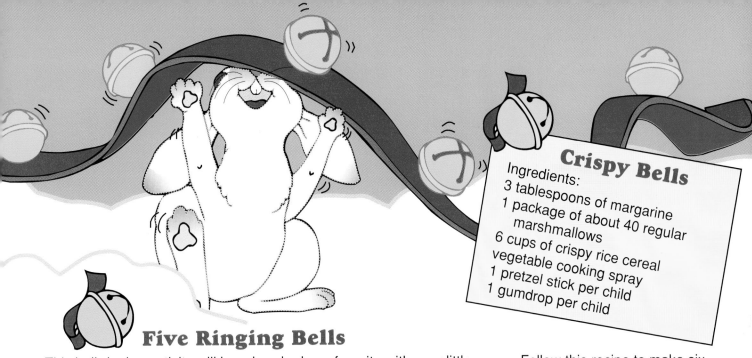

Crispy Bells

Ingredients:
3 tablespoons of margarine
1 package of about 40 regular marshmallows
6 cups of crispy rice cereal
vegetable cooking spray
1 pretzel stick per child
1 gumdrop per child

Five Ringing Bells

This bell-ringing activity will be a hands-down favorite with your little ones. In advance collect one glove for each child in your class (check your school's Lost and Found or a local thrift store). Sew a silver jingle bell to each fingertip of each glove. Have your students wear the gloves as you recite this poem together.

Five silver bells, ringing in the air. *Hold up five fingers.*
The first one said, "Ring me everywhere." *Hold up one finger.*
The second one said, "Ring me every day." *Hold up two fingers.*
The third one said, "Ring me on a sleigh." *Hold up three fingers.*
The fourth one said, "Ring me loud and clear." *Hold up four fingers.*
The fifth one said, "Wintertime is here!" *Hold up five fingers*
and shake hand.

Follow this recipe to make six crispy bells. Melt the margarine in a large saucepan over low heat. Stir in the marshmallows. When the marshmallows have melted, remove the pan from the heat. Add the rice cereal, stirring well. Allow the mixture to cool but not harden. Spray the inside of a nine-ounce plastic cup and a child's hands with vegetable spray. Have her fill the cup with the mixture. Have her push a gumdrop into the top of the mixture to resemble the bell clapper. After approximately ten minutes, carefully take the mixture out of the cup. Next have the child push a pretzel in the top of the bell to resemble the handle. These crispy bells are really swell!

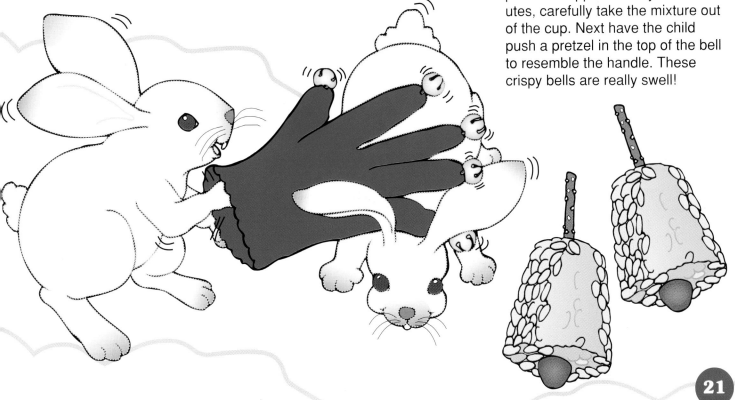

The Polar Express

In *The Polar Express* by Chris Van Allsburg (Houghton Mifflin Company), a boy boards a mysterious train that transports him to the North Pole. When Santa offers the boy any gift he desires, the boy asks him for a bell from a reindeer's harness. Read the book aloud; then present each child with a bell on a ribbon to wear. Remind the children that only if they believe in Santa will they hear the bells ring. Ring-a-ling! Do you believe?

Sleigh Ride

Oh, what fun it is to ride in this student-painted sleigh! Enlarge the sleigh pattern on page 23 onto a large piece of bulletin-board paper. Cut out the sleigh; then place it on the floor. Encourage children to paint the sleigh cutout with various colors of paint. When the sleigh is dry, tape it to two chairs that have been placed one behind the other. Place two additional chairs beside the first two chairs. Place one chair in front of the sleigh to represent a horse. To create reins, sew bells to two lengths of ribbon and tie the ribbon to the chair that represents the horse. Encourage students to sit on the chairs of the sleigh and hold onto the ribbon reins. With a little imagination, youngsters will soon be dashing through the snow!

All Aboard!

After reading aloud *The Polar Express* and distributing the bell necklaces, have students line up to form a train. Encourage youngsters to jingle their bells as you lead the train through the school. During your absence from the classroom, have an adult volunteer prepare a cup of warm cocoa for each child. When your crew arrives back at the classroom, have them sit down and enjoy the cocoa treat.

Books With Jingle

Jingle Bells: A Holiday Book With Lights And Music
Illustrated by Carolyn Ewing
Published by Aladdin Books

Jingle Bells
Written & Illustrated by Maryann Kovalski
Published by Little, Brown and Company

Jingle Bugs
Written & Illustrated by David Carter
Published by Simon & Schuster

Bells are really ringing in our class!

Please allow your child to bring a bell to school to share with the class.

Thank you!

_____

©The Education Center, Inc. • *December Holidays* • Preschool/Kindergarten • TEC3175

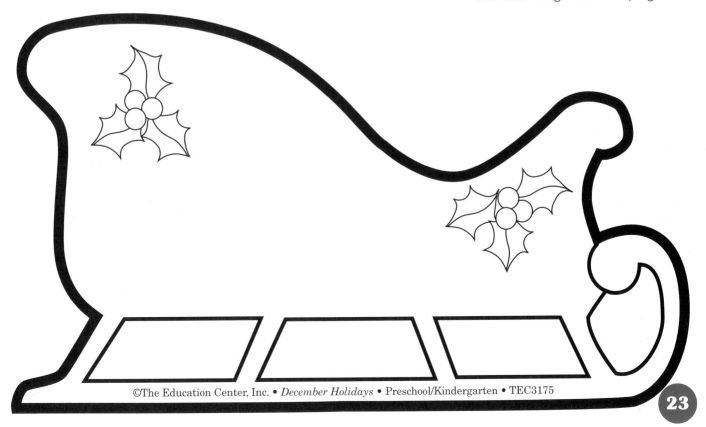

©The Education Center, Inc. • *December Holidays* • Preschool/Kindergarten • TEC3175

• • Bright Ideas • • • • •

Holiday Cheer

Parents will enjoy this unique gift idea that records your class's holiday cheer! Begin by audiotaping a holiday greeting to parents; then name each child in the class. During group times record your class singing their favorite holiday songs. When the tape is complete, duplicate a copy for each parent. Gift wrap the tapes and send one home with each child.

Kim Richman—Preschool
The Learning Zone
Des Moines, IA

Dreidel Delights

These delicious dreidels will leave youngsters spinning! To make one, insert one end of a pretzel stick into the center of a large marshmallow. Spread peanut butter onto the bottom of the marshmallow; then press the bottom of an unwrapped candy kiss onto the marshmallow. Spin, dreidel, spin!

Michelle Schwager—Preschool
St. Charles Center Care
Port Jefferson, NY

"Hand-y" Christmas Trees

Deck the halls with these terrific Christmas trees. To make a tree, press a hand into green tempera paint. Keeping the fingers and thumb close together, press the hand onto a sheet of white construction paper to represent tree leaves and branches. Cut a tree trunk from brown paper and glue it under the tree leaves. Then glue a gold or silver foil star to the top of the tree. To complete the project, use glitter glue, paint, or small candies to decorate the tree.

Tammy Bruhn—Pre-K
Ann Arbor, MI

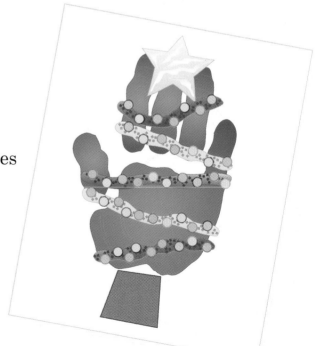

Holiday Gift Coupons

These coupon booklets are sure to be a hit with parents! Make two photocopies of an ornament pattern. Program one copy *Pick an ornament and you'll see / Just how helpful I can be*; then copy it for each child. Next make a supply of the unprogrammed ornament. On each of several copies, have each child illustrate herself helping with a different household chore. Then, if desired, assist her in labeling her illustrations. Staple each child's completed pages between construction paper covers; then have her decorate her front cover with seasonal cutouts or stickers. Little helpers will give these special gifts with pride!

Pat Gaddis—Pre-K
St. Timothy's Methodist Church School
Houston, TX

Recycling Trees

Save Christmas tree stumps to make name tags and provide a timely example of the *reusing* element of recycling. Cut each stump into circles of a desired thickness. Have each child sand a circle until it is smooth. (To avoid tiring, have children sand in several sittings.) On each wood circle, write a child's name; then drill a hole near the top. Apply a light coat of an acrylic sealer to the entire wood circle. When it is dry, thread a length of yarn or shoelace through the hole and tie the ends together to make a necklace.

Mary Lou Berg—Gr. K
Queen Of Peace School
Cloquet, MN

A Forest Of Decorated Firs

When these projects are displayed together, you'll have a fantastic forest of firs. To make a miniature fir tree, paint a pinecone with green tempera paint. Set the cone aside to dry. Following the package directions, mix a thick batch of plaster of paris. Drop a large spoonful of the mixture onto a piece of aluminum foil; then press the bottom of the pinecone into the plaster. When the plaster has set, embellish the fir tree by gluing on colorful beads.

Deborah Pruett, Woods Preschool
St. Mary Of The Woods College
St. Mary Of The Woods, IN

Add a festive seasonal flair to counting. Visually divide a bulletin board into sections using one-inch ribbon. Place a numeral cutout in each of the sections. Illustrate the numeral in each section using real or child-made holiday items such as ornaments, candy canes, dreidels, bells, holly leaves, and candles. Cut out letters traced onto holiday wrapping paper for the title of the board. Now you're counting holiday style!

Cathy Craze—Gr. K
Glade Creek Elementary School
Summersville, WV

Have each youngster cut out a shoe outline that he has traced onto brown paper and two hand outlines traced onto dark brown paper. Provide white and black construction-paper scraps for designing the eyes and crayons for drawing the mouth. Have youngsters glue the reindeer parts together. Assist each child in cutting a small circle just above his reindeer's mouth. Arrange red Christmas lights on a bulletin board background; then mount the reindeer so that the lights fit through the circles. If lights are not allowed in your school, glue on a red pom-pom for each reindeer's nose.

Robin Jory
Chaparral Elementary
Peoria, AZ

Magic Reindeer Mix

The bright light from Rudolph's nose is sure to help him find this magical reindeer mix! Mix some gold glitter into a container of dry oatmeal. Invite each child to scoop some reindeer mix into a personalized plastic sandwich bag. Attach a copy of the following note to each bag. Your little ones are sure to hear the pitter-patter of reindeer hooves racing to gobble up this tasty treat!

Kay Mayberry—Preschool
Good Shepherd Learning Center
Lafayette, IN

On Christmas Eve before you go to bed, sprinkle this magic reindeer food on your lawn. The magic glitter and the smell of the oats will help guide Rudolph to your house!

Call Rudolph!

Eight little reindeer pulling Santa's sled;

One fell down and bumped his head.

The elves called Santa and Santa said,

"Can seven little reindeer pull my sled?"

Seven little reindeer…
Six little reindeer…
Five little reindeer…
Four little reindeer…
Three little reindeer…
Two little reindeer…

One little reindeer pulling Santa's sled;
He fell down and bumped his head.
The elves called Santa and Santa said,
"Call Rudolph!"

(For reindeer finger puppets, please see page 48.)

(For reindeer finger puppets, please see page 48.)

—*dayle timmons*

Reindeer Shirts

Here's a "deer" gift that your little ones will proudly display—a reindeer T-shirt. In advance, purchase a white undershirt for each student and several cardboard T-shirt forms (found in most craft stores). Prewash each T-shirt. To make a reindeer shirt, stretch a shirt over a T-shirt form; then place it on the newspaper-covered floor. Have a student put one bare foot into a shallow pan of brown acrylic paint, then step onto the center of the shirt to make a footprint to represent a reindeer's head. After cleaning the paint from his foot, have the child place his hands in a pan of green acrylic paint and press his hands on either side of the reindeer's head to make handprint antlers. When the paint dries, have each youngster squeeze two dabs of slick fabric paint where the reindeer's eyes will be located, then press wiggle eyes atop the wet paint. Have him squeeze a dab of slick paint for the nose and press a large red sequin into the wet paint. To complete the project, use slick paint to personalize each child's shirt and add your name and the year. Repeat this process until each of your students has made a shirt.

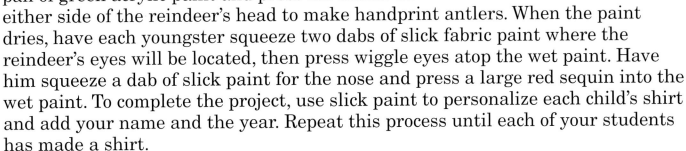

Maria Cuellar Munson
Preschool Unity Caring Club
Dallas, TX

Gifts That Measure Up

This festive holiday center really measures up! Have each youngster bring to school an empty box which has been wrapped in holiday gift wrap. To set up this center, place the wrapped boxes and a supply of rulers (for more advanced youngsters) beneath your classroom holiday tree. Have each youngster examine the boxes to determine the shortest, tallest, longest, biggest, and smallest. More advanced youngsters can measure the sides of the boxes with rulers and record the lengths. Youngsters will also enjoy sorting the packages by color or shape.

Bonnie Gaynor—Gr. K
Franklin Elementary School
Franklin, NJ

29

Sleep In Heavenly Peace

Melissa 2000

Sleep In Heavenly Peace

When sleeping on these pillows, your little ones will have the sweetest of dreams. Provide a prewashed, white pillowcase for each student, or ask each child to bring one. Before painting a pillowcase, insert a personalized sheet of paper that is the length and width of the pillowcase. Using fabric paint, generously paint a child's hand yellow or gold. Have her press her hand onto the pillowcase to form an angel's wings. After the child's hand has been washed and dried, paint it once more with a different color of her choice. Have her press her hand on the pillowcase again to form the angel's body. Using the appropriate colors, paint a head, hair, a halo, eyes, and a mouth. Add a message, the child's name, and the date. Add additional designs to the pillowcase if desired. Follow the manufacturer's instructions to permanently set the paints if necessary.

Janice Hughes and Jean Bower—Four- And Five-Year-Olds
Messiah Lutheran Nursery School
Williamsport, PA

Holiday Gift Tree

This display doubles as a great gift idea. Invite each child to use red and green ink-filled bingo markers to paint a white paper plate. Take a picture of each child; then trim the developed photos into circles. Glue each child's photo onto the center of his plate. Punch a hole near the top of the plate; then attach lengths of curling ribbon. Arrange the plates in a tree shape on a wall. Just before Christmas vacation, remove the plates from the wall, and send them home to parents.

Joan Johnson—Four-Year-Olds
Columbus School
Bridgeport, CT

Sweets For The Sweet

As they make these candies, visions of sugarplums and other sweet goodies will be dancing in the heads of your youngsters. To introduce the activity, show students an assortment of wrapped candies, and discuss the colors, designs, and wrappings. To make a piece of candy, glue two paper plates together, forming a disk shape. Once the glue has dried, paint the exposed surfaces of the plates to resemble a piece of candy. When the paint is dry, use plastic wrap to wrap the plates so that they look like wrapped candies. Use fishing line to suspend each youngster's candy creation from the ceiling.

Lenora Meyer—Gr.K
Ezra Millard School
Omaha, NE

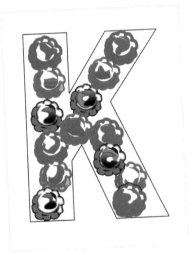

Kwanzaa Corn Craft

Here's a craft to help add meaning to your celebration of Kwanzaa. Break or cut an ear of corn into thirds. Prepare trays of red, black, and green tempera paint. Use the corn and paint to make creative prints on white construction paper. If desired, write a large *K* on a piece of paper. Print inside the outline of the letter with the corn. *K* is for Kwanzaa!

Dayle Timmons—Special Education Pre-K
Alimacani Elementary School
Jacksonville, FL

Eraser Counters

This activity can be easily adapted to address the time of year and the needs and interests of your children. On a page of a seasonal-shaped pad, write a number word or numeral, and/or draw an array of dots. Provide a supply of seasonal erasers for children to use as counters. Have each child match an eraser to each dot, or put the indicated amount of erasers on each shape-pad page.

Wendy Darcy
Waco, TX

The Reindeer Pokey

Round up all of your little reindeer for this holiday version of "The Hokey Pokey."

You put your antlers in. You put your antlers out.
You put your antlers in and you shake them all about.
You do the Reindeer Pokey and you turn yourself around.
That's what it's all about!

You put your hooves in....

You put your red nose in....

You put your fluffy tail in....

You put your reindeer body in....

Tara K. Moore
Hightower Elementary
Doraville, GA

Pass The Present

Youngsters will love this musical game that develops timing and hand-eye coordination. After all, the holidays *are* a time for giving—and giving, and giving! To prepare for play, gift wrap a small box for every two students. Pair students; then have them sit facing each other. Give one child in each pair a present. Have the children practice passing the gift back and forth. Next have them pass the gift each time you play a note on a set of bells. Have them continue to pass the gift as you play a steady beat on the bells. As a challenge increase the tempo of your steady beat. As a variation for older preschoolers, have youngsters pass one gift around a group circle as you play a steady beat.

five candy canes

and a little, teeny, tiny, candy bear.

"The Twelve Days Of Christmas"

Add a creative flair to your holiday festivities with these student-made booklets. After familiarizing your youngsters with "The Twelve Days Of Christmas," encourage them to create their own versions. Beginning approximately three weeks before Christmas vacation, have each youngster illustrate the first verse of his version of the song. Assist each child in labeling his page. Daily thereafter for 11 more days, have each child illustrate the succeeding verses. When all 12 pages are complete, staple each child's set between construction paper covers. Add the title _____'s *Twelve Days Of Christmas* to his front cover before having him decorate it. For added fun, join each youngster in singing his new version of this old favorite.

Tanya Wheeler
Pelahatchie Elementary
Pelahatchie, MS

Tabletop Menorah

Sharpen your children's patterning skills with this enlightening suggestion! Use masking tape or colored tape to make a menorah design on a tabletop. Have your children create their own unique patterns along the design using a variety of math counters. As you admire a student's work, ask her to describe the attribute she used for patterning. Your little ones will light up when it's their turn at this festive center!

Nancy Barad—Four-Year-Olds
Bet Yeladim Preschool And Kindergarten
Columbia, MD

Holiday Parent Workshop

Invite parents to a holiday workshop with activities that are not only fun, but also provide opportunities for positive interaction and language development as well. Prior to the workshop, have your students help you decorate your classroom. Then organize learning centers with a holiday theme. For example, you might want to prepare centers in which parents and children listen to a story, make ornaments, and follow directions to decorate cookies. Encourage all of the children and parents to use the ornaments they made to decorate a tree together. Conclude the workshop by eating the cookies and by singing holiday songs. As they are headed out the door, provide parents with a copy of any patterns or recipes that they used in the centers. A good time will be had by all!

Cathie Pesa—Preschool Special Needs
Youngstown City Schools
Youngstown, OH

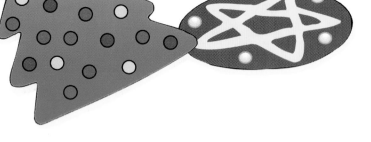

"Toy-rific" Tree

Looking for a fun way to decorate your classroom Christmas tree? If so, then look no further than the toys on your classroom shelves. Simply string beads or connect Learning Links® to make colorful garlands. Twist pipe cleaners around toy animals, DUPLO® people, bear counters, or other small manipulatives. Then hang the items on the tree. Place a star-shaped manipulative on the top for a tree that's totally "toy-rific"!

Amy Deml—Preschool
Mary Of Lourdes Community Preschool
Little Falls, MN

Once Upon A Holiday Book...

What could be better on a winter's day than settling down with a good book? Designate a day during the holiday season for students to come to school in their pajamas or wear pajamas under their clothes. (Don't forget to put on your own bathrobe and slippers!) Encourage youngsters to also bring stuffed toys, pillows, and blankets to school on that day. To create the perfect atmosphere for a cozy reading time together, dim the lights and play soft music. Gather all of your youngsters around you and, once everyone is cozy, read aloud selections of holiday literature such as *The Polar Express* and *'Twas The Night Before Christmas*. After several selections, everyone can settle down for a long winter's nap!

Marsha Feffer—Pre-K
Salem Early Childhood Center
Salem, MA

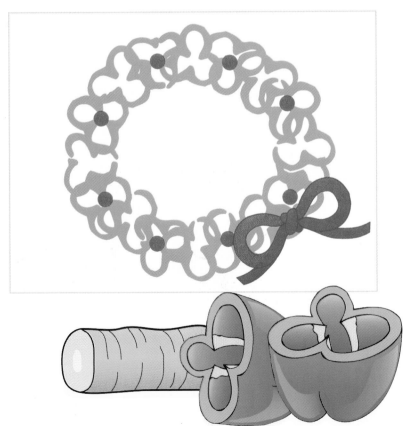

Pepper Wreath

Spruce up your room with these pepper wreaths. In advance, cut a pepper in half and remove the seeds. Also cut a carrot in half. To make a wreath, draw a circle on a large sheet of art paper. Dip a pepper-half into one shade of green paint; then repeatedly press it onto the circle outline, creating a design that resembles a wreath. Repeat this process using the other pepper-half and another shade of green paint. Then dip a carrot-half in red paint and randomly press it onto the wreath to resemble berries. When the paint is dry, glue a red bow to the wreath.

Sandie Bolze—Gr. K
Verne Critz Elementary School
East Patchogue, NY

Christmas Tree Treats

This yummy Christmas tree is as much fun to make as it is to eat. To make a tree, use a plastic knife to cover the outside of a sugar cone with vanilla frosting. Gently press small candy pieces—such as M&M's®, Skittles®, or nonpareils—into the frosting. These delectable trees are bound to bring smiles to your youngsters' faces.

Robbin Kearley
Northeast Elementary
Greenwell Springs, LA

Kwanzaa Candles

Use this poem as a fingerplay or to introduce a real *kinara* (candleholder) and the *mishumaa saba* (seven candles) used during Kwanzaa.

Seven little candles all in a line,
Waiting to be lighted at Kwanzaa time.
Come let's count them—one, two, three,
Four, five, six, seven candles I see!

Christina Yuhouse—Preschool
New Horizons School
Latrobe, PA

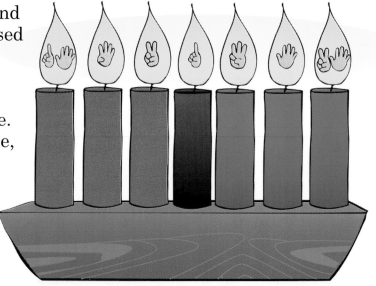

Reproducible Activities...

Holiday Rhymes

How To Use Pages 38–40

1. Make a class supply of the cookie pattern on this page and pages 39–40.
2. After each child completes the directions on pages 39 and 40, have him color the pictures, then cut on the bold outlines. Supply each child with a cookie pattern; then have him cut it out.
3. Assist each student in gluing the cookie cutout between the two gingerbread cutouts as shown.

Finished Sample

Cookie Patterns

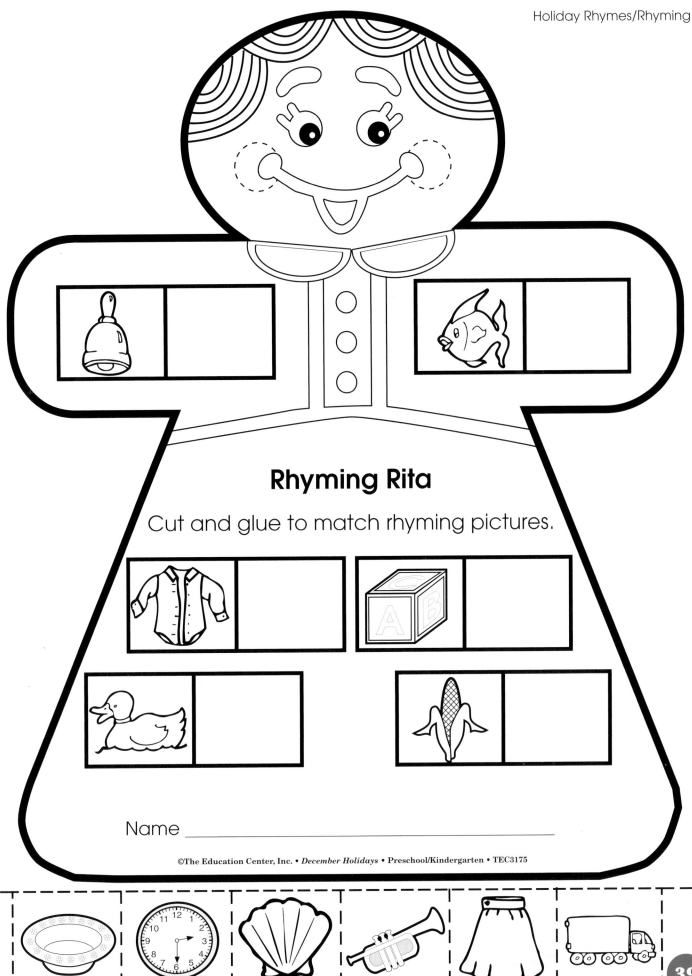

Rhyming Rita

Cut and glue to match rhyming pictures.

Name _____

©The Education Center, Inc. • *December Holidays* • Preschool/Kindergarten • TEC3175

39

Rhyming Roy

Cut and glue to match rhyming pictures.

Name _____

©The Education Center, Inc. • *December Holidays* • Preschool/Kindergarten • TEC3175

Name _____

Pile Of Presents

Find the rhyme in each box.

Color the pictures that rhyme.

Latkes And Applesauce
Literature Unit

Story Synopsis
Latkes And Applesauce

Latkes And Applesauce by Fran Manushkin (published by Scholastic Inc.) is a warm and appealing story of a loving family and how their kindness to a stray kitten and dog brings them joy as they celebrate Hanukkah.

How To Use Page 43

1. Duplicate the page for each child.
2. Read *Latkes And Applesauce* aloud to your children.
3. After discussing the story, call attention to each of the pictures on the right side of the page. Ask each child to decide which pictures show things that apply to Latke, the dog, and which pictures show things that apply to Applesauce, the cat.
4. Have each child color and cut out the pictures, then glue them in the boxes below the characters.
5. Have each child draw a flame above each of the candles in the menorah.

Finished Sample

Name Abby

Story Characters

Listen to the story.
Color. Cut. Glue.

Latke	Applesauce
drumstick	milk
hole	tree
potatoes	apples

Color to light the candles.

Name _____

Latkes And Applesauce/Literature

Story Characters

Listen to the story.
 Color. ✂ Cut.  Glue.

🐕 Latke	🐈 Applesauce

🖍 Color to light the candles.

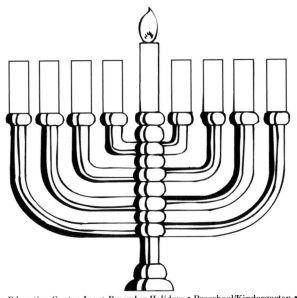

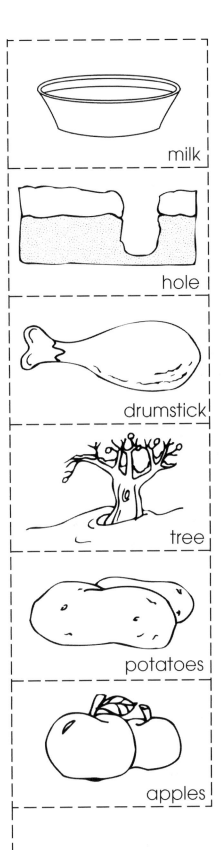

milk

hole

drumstick

tree

potatoes

apples

©The Education Center, Inc. • December Holidays • Preschool/Kindergarten • TEC3175

43

Hanukkah

How To Use Page 45

1. Read aloud the following directions to guide students in completion of the sheet:

   - *Look at the first box. This special candle holder is called a* menorah. *During Hanukkah, families light the candles from left to right. A new candle is lighted each night of the holiday, using the center candle to light the others. Circle the center candle of the menorah.*

   - *Look at the next box. Families enjoy special foods during the holidays. During Hanukkah, families enjoy* latkes, *or potato pancakes. Color the potato pancakes or latkes brown.*

   - *Look at the next box. Special games are played during the holidays. Children enjoy playing* dreidel *during Hanukkah. A dreidel is a top. Color the dreidel yellow.*

   - *Look at the last picture. Gifts are exchanged during Hannukah. Find the biggest gift in the picture. Draw a bow for this gift and decorate the wrapping paper.*

2. If desired, have children color the sheet.

Finished Sample

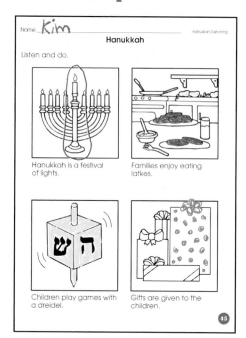

Hanukkah

Listen and do.

Hanukkah is a festival of lights.

Families enjoy eating latkes.

Children play games with a dreidel.

Gifts are given to the children.

How To Use Page 47

1. Make a supply of the patterns on construction paper. (Keep in mind that each page contains four pairs.)
2. Color the pictures if desired; then program each of the open spaces with a skill. For example, program each of the ornaments with a numeral and each of the trees with a set of dots. Laminate the pages; then cut apart the cards.
3. Store all of the cards in a string-tie envelope. (If desired, enlarge and duplicate one copy of each pattern to color and glue onto the string-tie envelope.)
4. To use the activity cards, a child takes all of the cards out of the string-tie envelope, then matches each tree to an ornament.

Variations

• Make a supply of the patterns. Color each of the patterns so that they can be used for patterning activities. Laminate the patterns; then cut them out. Have youngsters create repeating patterns with the cards and duplicate each other's patterns.

• Make a supply of the patterns. Program them with the sequencing skills of your choice. Have youngsters arrange the cards in order.

• Make a supply of the patterns; then cut them apart. Keep them in a handy place so that, just at the right moment, you'll be able to grab one of the cards and write a personalized message to reward and/or encourage a specific child.

• Make a supply of the patterns; then cut them apart. Use them as nametags or for short notes.

Holiday Activity Cards

Reindeer Finger Puppets

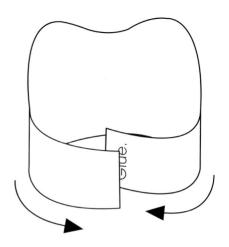

How To Use This Page
1. Duplicate the patterns below on construction paper for sturdiness.
2. Have children color the reindeer.
3. Instruct each child to cut out the reindeer along the dotted lines.
4. Apply glue along the left edge of each puppet and roll the strip to form the ring of the finger puppet.
5. Use the puppets to sing a favorite reindeer song or fingerplay.